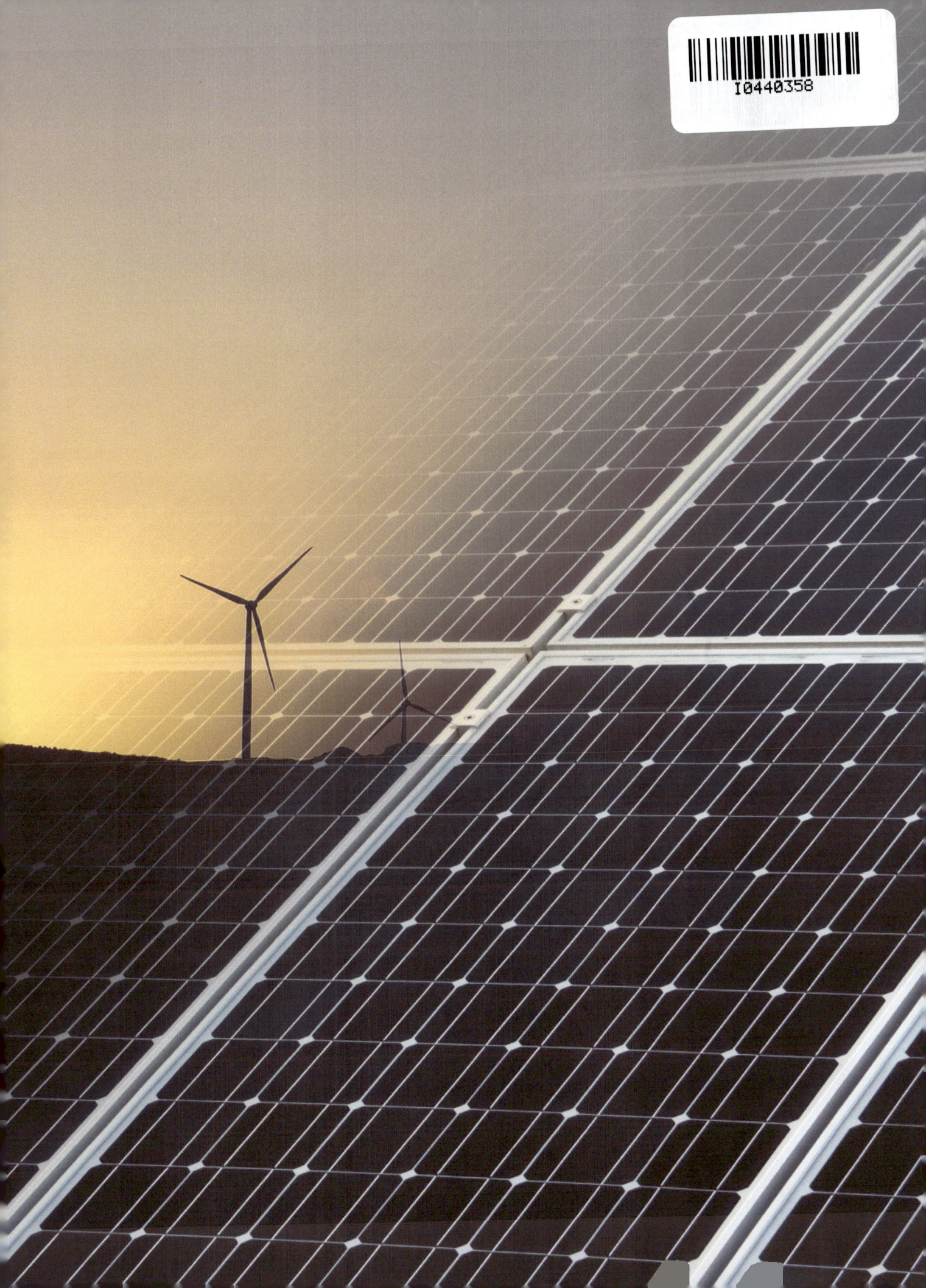

©Trinidad and Tobago Climate Network 2023
Design by Katrina Khan-Roberts

ISBN: 9798867747176
Independently Published

For information about custom editions, sales and premium and corporate purchases please contact Katrina Khan-Roberts at 1-868-480-5378 or tntclimatenetwork@gmail.com.

Created in Trinidad and Tobago
November 2023

Perspectives of Trinidad and Tobago on the Just Transition

An Artistic and Literary Anthology

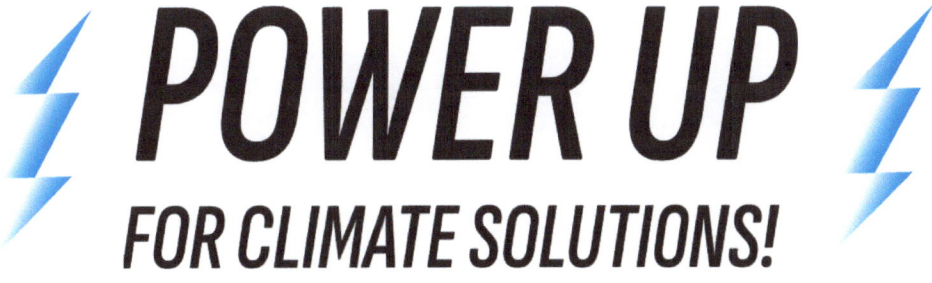

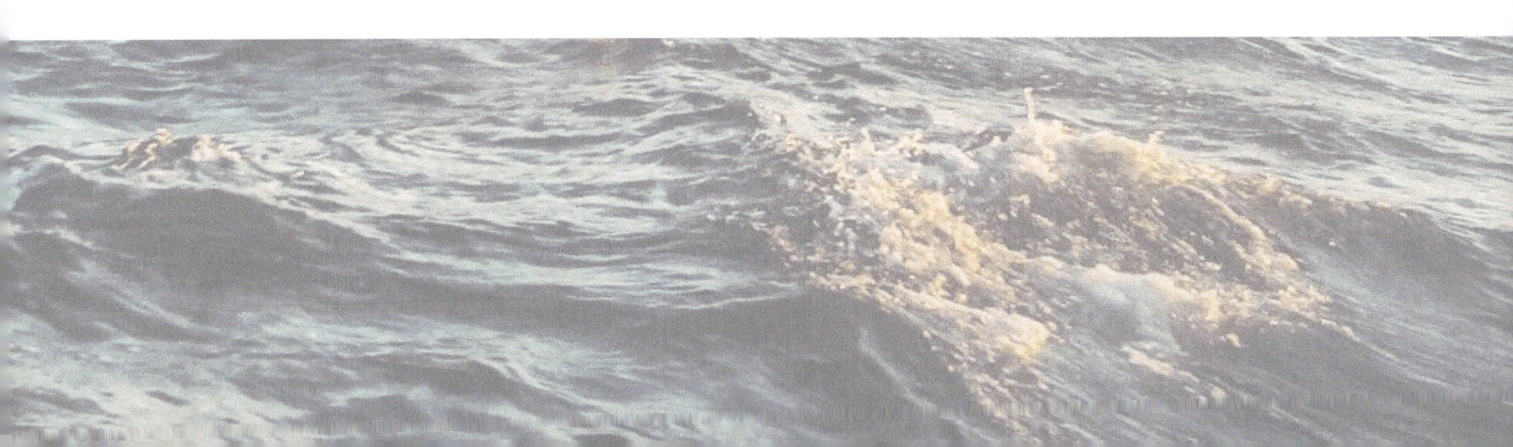

This book is a compilation of the 2023 submissions for the Power Up action in Trinidad and Tobago, organised by the Trinidad and Tobago Climate Network.

We must look beyond awareness and to solutions building in the face of an escalating climate crisis.

Equip yourselves with knowledge and be guided by good ethics towards a better future for all.

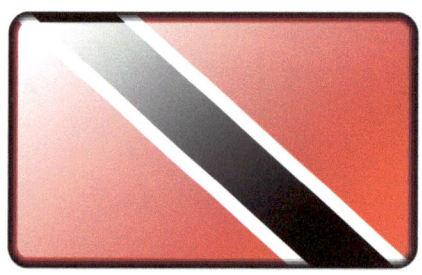

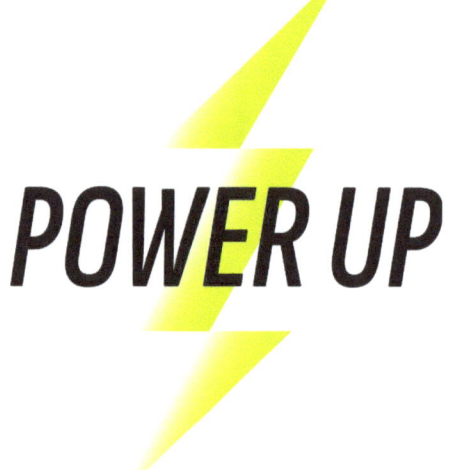

About Power Up

Power Up is a global initiative led by 350.org and partners who joined forces with local movements, groups and communities (like ours) to spotlight the oil industry's greed and reclaim the money to fund a just and equitable future powered by clean energy.

In November 2023, all around the world, people came together to power up the global renewable energy revolution. In Trinidad and Tobago, we raised our voices through art and creativity. Our thoughts, hopes, and the solutions we demand from our leaders are contained in this Anthology.

A bit about the Editor

Katrina Khan-Roberts is a Tourism, Health, Safety and Environment professional with special interest in the sustainable development of human society in tandem with nature. She advocates actively for awareness of climate change, sustainable development and holistic lifestyle.

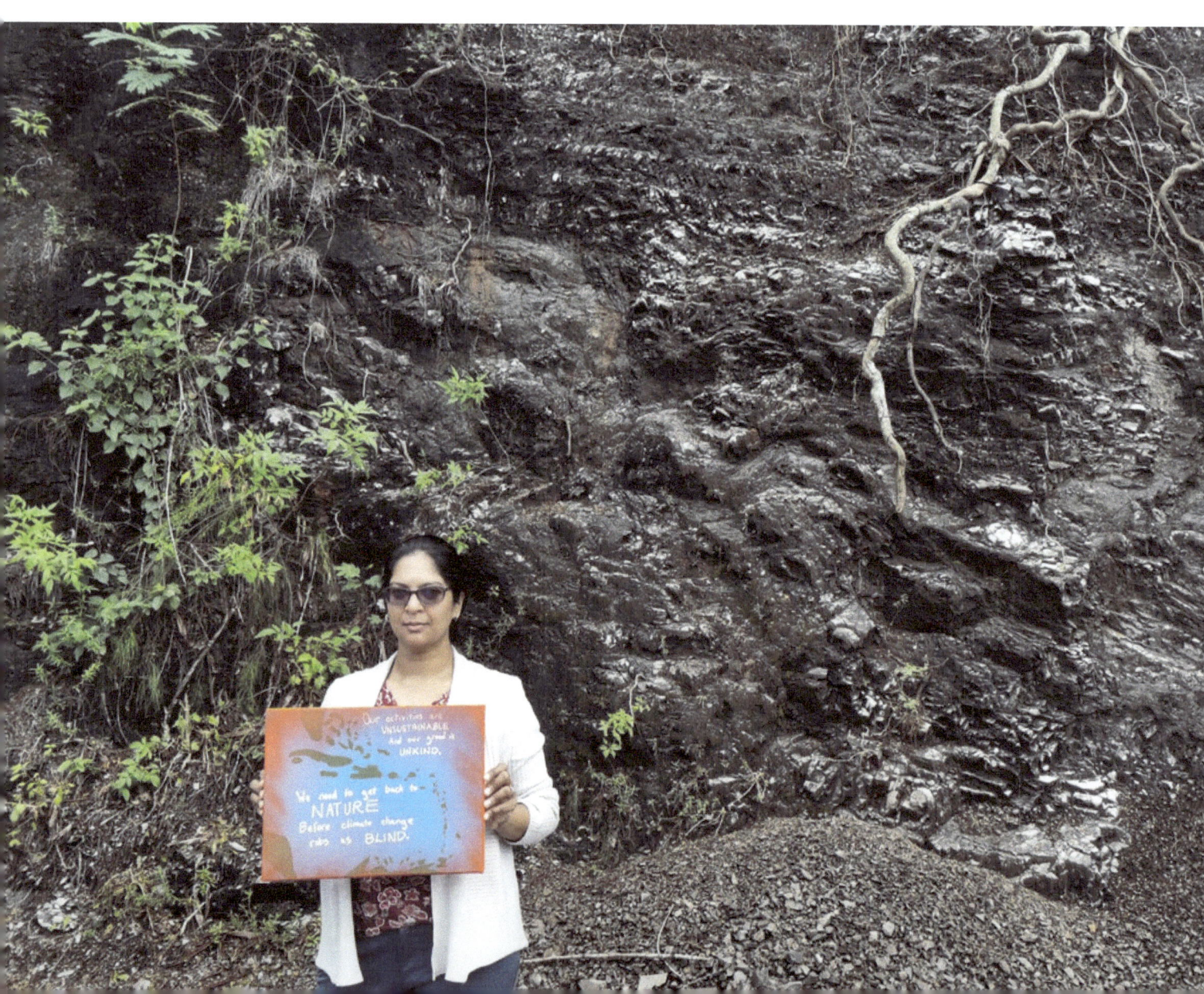

The Caribbean Climate Network and
the Trinidad and Tobago Climate Network

We are a group of climate advocates from the Caribbean region who are working together to push for actions that protect our communities against the impacts of the climate crisis.

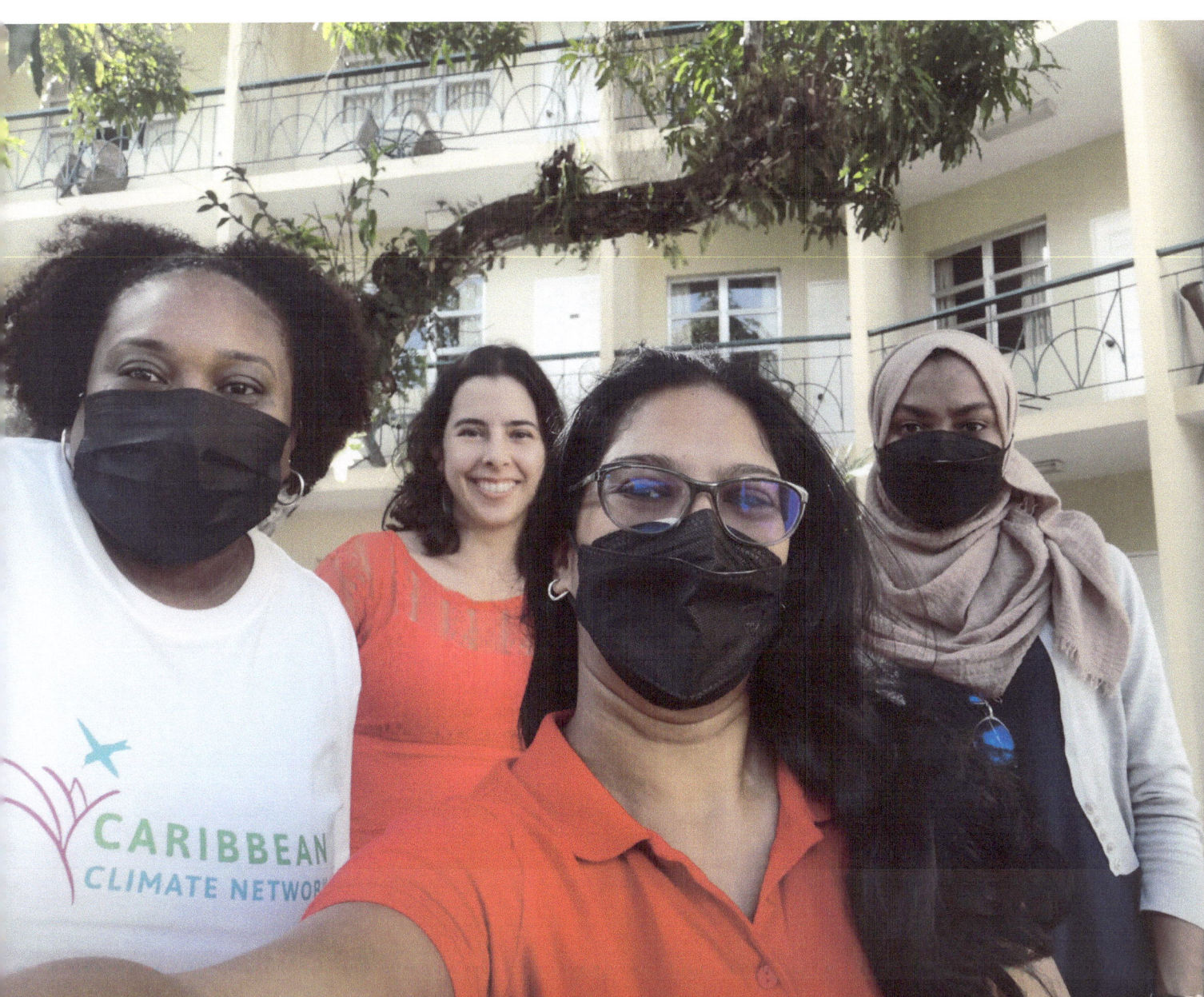

Foreward

What is the Just Transition in T&T?

The Silesia Declaration, adopted by acclamation at the 24th Conference of the Parties to the UNFCCC provides a clear mandate for "a Just Transition of the workforce and the creation of decent work and quality jobs, in accordance with nationally defined development priorities."

The transition to a low-carbon future has a global dimension that impacts all actors in society, from governments to businesses to individuals. As a result, it is essential to guarantee a Just Transition to improve societal welfare and achieve climate goals.

Just Transition is defined as "a bridge from where we are today to a future where all jobs are green and decent, poverty is eradicated, and communities are thriving and resilient." More precisely, it is a systemic and whole economy approach to sustainability.

A Just Transition is instrumental in achieving long-term national and climate goals to ensure that no one is left behind, preserve environmental integrity, and protect the rights of vulnerable populations and future generations.

An energy transition will include new opportunities such as promoting renewables, new mobility services, and sustainable agricultural models. However, it also means the disappearance of some sectors, such as fossil-fuel-based industries, which Trinidad and Tobago is dependent on, with knock-on effects on manufacturing sectors.

The average cost of electricity generation with new solar photovoltaic plants dropped by 75% between 2010 and 2017. Renewables are the cheapest form of new power generation in many parts of the world. The trend of global investment in renewable energy is increasing, while investments are divesting from fossil fuels.

The new jobs created by the transition are described by the ILO as "not just the creation of jobs, but also the creation of jobs of acceptable quality." This means a worker in a waning sector needs to be able to find similar work in the green economy. A justice focused transition will lower the risk of stranded assets and jobs.

Gender equality must be addressed in the Just Transition and ensure that training and jobs available in the green industries are equally accessible for women as men and that women and girls are not left behind due to existing conditions and inequalities.

As a fossil fuel-rich economy, T&T has the 19th highest GDP per capita in the Americas. Low electricity rates and fuel subsidies give few incentives to develop renewables or energy efficiency technologies. Its contribution to global emissions is below 0.1%, but with its small population it has one of the highest per capita emissions.

Trinidad and Tobago's vision is to harmonize its climate, energy, and economic goals through a Just Transition to a low-carbon pathway to provide equal opportunity to all members of society. By making the low carbon transition fair, it addresses economic, social, and environmental goals along with the Sustainable Development Goals (SDGs).

The Just Transition Policy's goal is to become a framework for T&T to achieve its vision of harmonizing its climate, energy, and economic goals through a move to a low-carbon pathway. It will guide using governance instruments, strategies, and policies to provide a clear vision of what needs to be achieved in a Just Transition.

Society United Now

Hassan Voyeau

<u>October 13, 2023</u>

I went out for lunch today. I walked in the blazing midday sun. Beads of sweat drained from my sun tanned forehead. The air condition in the food shop struggles to keep the room cool. I think to myself that imagine we are in the rainy season now. What will happen in the dry season? I was chatting with a friend and he asked if this was climate change and I agreed.

And as God would have it, I was scrolling through facebook and came across an art and writing challenge where the topic is Perspectives of Trinidad and Tobago on the Just Transition. The message from God was clear, this is your chance to make a difference. According to the ILO website, a Just Transition involves maximizing the social and economic opportunities of climate action, while minimizing and carefully managing any challenges. I decided to lend my voice to this effort by doing what I am good at, blogging. I decided to be creative with the title and spell out sun as society united now.

One way I imagine progress being made is by each of us doing what we can. Our voices and actions together will create momentum that will get the attention of the decision makers. There is a trini saying that goes "stone in water doh know when sun hot" and I think that will be our biggest challenge. How do we get the powerful persons in society who we imagine are insulated from the current effects of climate change to join the movement and take action now.

Climate change is real, it is one of our big problems and we have to act now. We need easily achievable consensus and action that starts from you and me and the home to the community to the country to the world. We need a united front to take on the battle of climate change. We should not let it reach the point where it becomes burn to learn. It certainly feels like that is happening though because I was surely burning in the sun today. The bright side though is that if we act right now then future generations would not have to burn to learn.

Trinidad and Tobago's Voyage Towards a Just Transition

Heidi Boodoosingh

" We delight in the beauty of the butterfly, but rarely admit the changes it has gone through to achieve that beauty. "
-Maya Angelou

In the midst of the sapphire waters of a twin-island known as Trinidad and Tobago, where the prevalent trade winds fill the surroundings with tropical breeze, a nation arrives at a crucial fork in the road. The bright side blossoming with innovation, resilience, sustainability and hope, mirrored by the bleak setting of an era fueled by fossil fuels. Trinidad and Tobago is invited to set out on a road to become a carbon-neutral economy. This change embodies the hopes and aspirations of a country resolute in redefining its course towards a more equitable and sustainable future.

The oil and gas sector has long been connected with the Republic of Trinidad and Tobago and has had a significant impact on the development of the nation's economy and society. However, despite these decades of wealth and economic prosperity generated by the oil and gas sector, the world is now facing the unforgiving specter of climate change and the winds of change are altering our course.

As the world wrestles with the paramount need to confront climate change and transition towards more sustainable and ecologically responsible mannerisms, the idea of a "just transition" has ascended to prominence. The Just transition framework, is articulated as "a bridge from where we are today to a future where all jobs are green and decent, poverty is eradicated, and communities are thriving and resilient." It works to guarantee that the transition from an economy based on fossil fuels to one that is greener, more sustainable, and equitable does not disproportionately hurt workers or communities who are already disadvantaged. Trinidad and Tobago stand poised, ready to embrace a future that must be sustainable, just, and free from the chains of fossil fuels in this dance of reinvention.

Historically, T&T has been heavily dependent on the energy sector, particularly oil and gas. Although these resources have contributed to the nation's wealth, the country's economy has also become reliant on the prices and demand for these fossil fuels in the global market. When global energy prices rise, the nation benefits, but when they fall, the economy can suffer. This vulnerability to unpredictable fluctuations in global energy markets is a risk that the country faces due to its heavy reliance on these resources. As such, this dependency of fossil fuels poses a significant challenge to the long-term sustainability of the country, since fossil fuels contribute greatly to greenhouse gas emissions and is subjected to risks associated with a swiftly changing energy sector.

And so, "the winds of change are altering our course". Trinidad and Tobago's journey towards a carbon-neutral or journey toward vastly reducing our carbon footprint is paved with innovation. Many have recognized the significance of transitioning to a more diversified and sustainable economy. We see the 'just transition' framework as an opportunity to invest or investigate alternative industries such as exploring renewable energy sources, agribusiness, eco-tourism and new innovative, sustainable technology. Our STEM workers and researchers, now labor to come up with resourceful, environmentally conscious ways to harness the bountiful renewable resources that nature provides us with, as well as come up with technology to enhance the efficiency and sustainability of agribusiness, as well as promote the preservation and rehabilitation of our natural ecosystems.

Just transition is not solely about embracing renewables and embarking on a journey towards sustainable technology and environmental preservation; it is also about ensuring that no one is left behind. The concept of just transition emphasizes the need to protect vulnerable communities and laborers who may be adversely affected by the transition away from fossil fuels to a more sustainable carbon-neutral energy approach. It is perceived that an equitable transition can be achieved by providing job opportunities in multiple sectors for those who have been misplaced as a result of the transition by providing them with the opportunities for reskilling and reemployment in the emerging, transitional sectors, as well as provide an array of jobs for additional persons, and so cause a decrease in employment and improve the rate of poverty in the nation.

As the nation charts its path, a sense of environmental responsibility also emerges. The implementation of this just transition policy will require the involvement of all government ministries and agencies as well as the public swaying together with a world that trembles for sustainability. They need to understand that this shift can reduce the country's carbon footprint and aid in the protection of the environment, including the delicate ecosystems in and around the Caribbean and must assist in implementing strategies, as sustainability is a team sport that can only be achieved if we all join forces to save the planet just as we have unconsciously joined forces to hurt the planet.

Like a waltz, the road to transition is filled with many spins and dips. Waltzing away from the firm grasp of fossil fuels could lead us to a path of economic vulnerability or uncertainty. The energy sector has been a reliable source of revenue and employment for Trinidad and Tobago and the development of new markets and industries would take some time as well as require a large investment. Another short-coming of the just transition concept is that transitioning communities and workers may falter in the shift so there must be strategies put in place to ensure a seamless transition from one era to another. Additionally, there may be individuals who would put up a resistance toward the transition, fearing the loss of economic influence or just due to the ignorance of refusing to see the bigger picture and in this instance, overcoming the resistance may require a coordinated approach of policy-making, implementation and public engagement.

Yet, despite the challenges, home in our diverse Caribbean island of Trinidad and Tobago we have a wide array of opportunities to "just transition". For instance, being a tropical country as Trinbago is located near the equator, sunlight is abundant throughout the year making it the ideal location for solar energy generation. Similarly, Trinidad and Tobago also has the potential for wind energy generation as we are an island so we are surrounded by coastline and coastal areas are often exposed to steady, strong and frequently occurring trade winds which are ideal for the harnessing and generation of wind energy. These resources can be harnessed for export and domestic growth. Transitioning can also result in building relationships between international partners and organizations supporting the same cause and these collaborations can result in more opportunities for funding and additional expertise and technology that would be able to facilitate the transition. The transition would also offer opportunities for local research and development in sustainability practices.

"The mushroom is a symbol of nature's transformative power, reminding us that even in the darkest places, growth and renewal are always possible."
-Sweetellabella

Perspectives on a just transition in Trinidad and Tobago reflect an understanding of the importance of sustainability and environmental responsibility. Despite the short-term difficulties associated with this framework, there are huge chances to reconstruct the country's economy and society in a way that is more equitable and ecologically beneficial

A just transition represents not only an economic and environmental narrative but also a chance for Trinidad and Tobago to build a more resilient and sustainable future adorn in prosperity. It serves as an anthem for a future that is brighter, cleaner, and more just.

Heidi Boodoosingh

Choose Your Future!

Mikhaela Browne

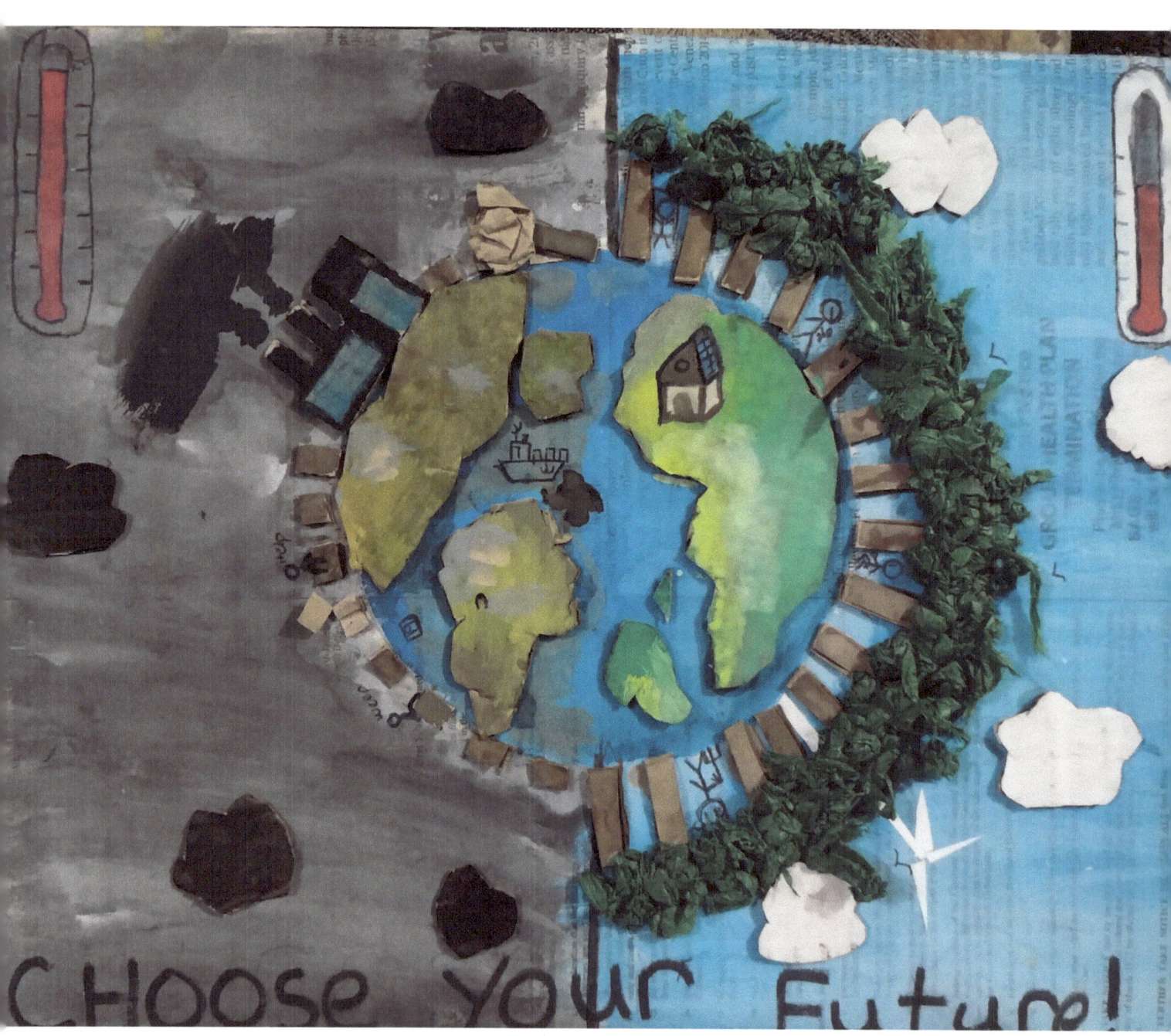

A Letter From The Future

Ryan Bachoo

Hello Trinidad and Tobago,

Greetings from the year 2050. If you were here, it would be difficult to recognise your own country. The government is on a desperate hunt for gas reserves to jumpstart the economy. Oil has stopped flowing and now it's dripping but it hardly matters because most of the world has stopped buying it anyway. The local oil and gas industry is suffering and engineers are fleeing.

They're not the only ones. Fishermen are struggling. Trinidad's waters are warming and fishes are dying. The price of fish has skyrocketed. Cascadura, catfish and barracudas don't visit these shores anymore. Fishermen on the north coast protesting saying the government failed to protect their livelihood from global warming.

They demanding compensation and relocation because rising sea levels beginning to erode the coastlines. Houses are cracking. Some of them falling. Families begging. Children crying.

It's not only fish, it's the entire dish. Farmers bemused by the lack of balance in weather patterns. One month, the heat killing their livestock. It doesn't have enough water to wet their crops. Next month, violent rainfall and floods. Acres of produce under water.

The country struggling to decide whether it prefers sun or rain. Too much sun and WASA reservoirs running low. Protests from Penal to Port of Spain for water. Too much rain, houses and businesses being flooded again and again.

One man on TV say, "So nobody saw this coming?" A woman preaching on High Street say, "Prepare for the second coming."

Tobago tourism struggling so they call for a referendum to get out of this twin-island situation. Venezuelan businesses booming but the US ease sanctions so they looking to head back to their nation.

Climate change affecting everything. Scientists saying we told you so. Politicians pointing fingers to leaders from 30 years ago.

Let this be a warning T&T. You all headed to a serious disparity. To transition is a must, but it doesn't have to be just.

Yours respectfully,
The year 2050.

The Trinbagonian Cycle of Just Transition

Davi Ramkallawan

Climate change, pollution, energy, nations, governments, big businesses
All in this cycle of just transition
Clean, green and serene a toil for all
Providing opportunities for fruitful discussion and action
With far reaching impact and societal gains
Our sustainability..our livelihood
Must endure fair negotiation

We as a people cry out for justice
Like every creed and race find an equal place
So must Trinbagonian citizens when they set out to establish their place
In an ever-changing economy controlled by energy
We must do better, be more resilient in this fight to restore
Lest we lose our pride and joy that we wear so eloquently
The red, white and black synonymous with our powerful global impact
So deep within our spirit it implores us to improve
Minimizing waste and pollution whilst protecting our fragile ecosystem

Adaptation is key to restoration
Our environment, the playground for change and difference makers
Green jobs, raw material efficiency and renewable energy
In every sector especially agriculture
Not forgetting those who manufacture
Clean production processes with best practices help just transition
Especially in workspaces where everyone is mandated to get their act together with
Occupational health and safety a must
To reduce accidents and incidents for workers, organizations and societal
expectations
Highlighting each on an equal footing is just

This call is received far and wide by rural and urban societies within all countries
Being environment friendly is everyone's responsibility
From the air and water we drink..our elixir of life
To the food we eat, clothes we wear and distinguished movements all leave indelible
footprints
That tell our stories to future generations
As Darwin so wisely surmised on natural selection and human evolution
We are all interrelated in this fight for existence which heavily depends on our
change
management

A bit of mindfulness goes a long way in reducing, reusing, recycling and upcycling
What is good for the mind and body, is good for the environment and economy
So let's play our part
However big or small a ripple it may be in the pond of life
Where profiteering, flooding, overheating and the rising cost of living seem to
strangle
our small voices
Let's target our actions to the future and a better tomorrow
The struggle is real but we must endure
The sun, the wind, the ocean and land have become our evil nemesis
The time is now..a call for action to fight this looming climate crisis
Let them pay up or power up
With all this education, advocation and government supplication we will surely
elevate
Our united voice where none can eradicate

Davi Ramkallawan

Heated Earth

Lee-Marie Preston

The Earth
Take a look around
It's a wonderful space
Not one leaf falls into a spot out of place

The beautiful mountains and riverlets
The beaches and sunsets
Those same beaches that attract tourists
The heat that they want to hide from the cold
The same heat
That we treat
Like we want to disown

Every single day
We are caught in dismay
Driven away
From the heat appeal
That others want to feel

But we cause the earth harm
Try to wash away its calm nature
Destroying the ozone layer
And disarm
Ourselves

Defense-less from the sun rays
But we complain anyway
As if we aren't the ones that increase the heat
And influence the rate
At which global warming occurs

We disregard the warning signs
The over powering hot weather rushes to an incline
The rainfall is put into forceful drive
And we wonder why?

All the vehicles burning gas
The plastic bottles and sprawled trash
The destruction of trees
For the construction of roads that don't pass
A maximum of three days
And we want our Earth to last?
Let's cut down on using fossil fuels
Because even though we think that is what fuels our economy
It's demolishing the normal temperature constantly
The industries transition
But still don't find a better way to discard their emissions
And we fall into submission
Of the sun

We must make it our mission
Our most important assignment
Whether in school, working or in retirement
To conserve the world's energy
And preserve its resources
So lets make it a tendency
To choose solar power
Plant some more trees
Help our world flower

Help reduce the heat on Earth
Because both we and it are worth,
Saving
And then take some time
To absorb the world around
Cause the perfect creatures
And features are absolutely profound

Lee-Marie Preston

Who Dares?

I-yana Dinzey

Oh dear, sweet sweet Trinidad
Oh dear, sweet sweet Tobago
Oh dear sweet sweet Caribbean
a place place where you can jump
and jive, and loose up yuhself
but maybe that loose up, loosened
what makes us one.

Ah Unity!

a unity so strong where young and
old feel just alike, where one can
feel heard
but it seems like these days no
one is listening
and as the cradle of climate change
rocks bak and forth, and back and forth,
who do we see nurturing it?

US

Every single face of the human race.
and as it suckles on our breast, a dark
cloud looms over us that can one day ruin us all,
but we, we can change our fate.
come together as one government,
one society
one nation.

Oh dare,
Oh dare.

Red, Yellow, Green means Go!
Ayesha Rivers and Myalee Phillip

Green means go
Green represents nature
Nature is life
Life needs energy
energy to thrive
Thrive towards the future
a future where green means go

Yellow means slow
slow down and think
Think about the environment we live in.
Where should your trash be?
In our roads or in our bins
ever thought of recycling!
Now that you know, try and do so
Remember kids, Yellow means slow

Red means stop!
Stop emitting greenhouse gases
Stop killing our animals by the masses
Stop releasing your waste in our oceans
Stop dumping your waste in our lands
Stop chopping down our trees
Stop destroying our future
Stop denying a chance to save us
So let's all live within a nation where

Red means stop.

The Trinidad Road to Just Transition

Jayda Ramjattan

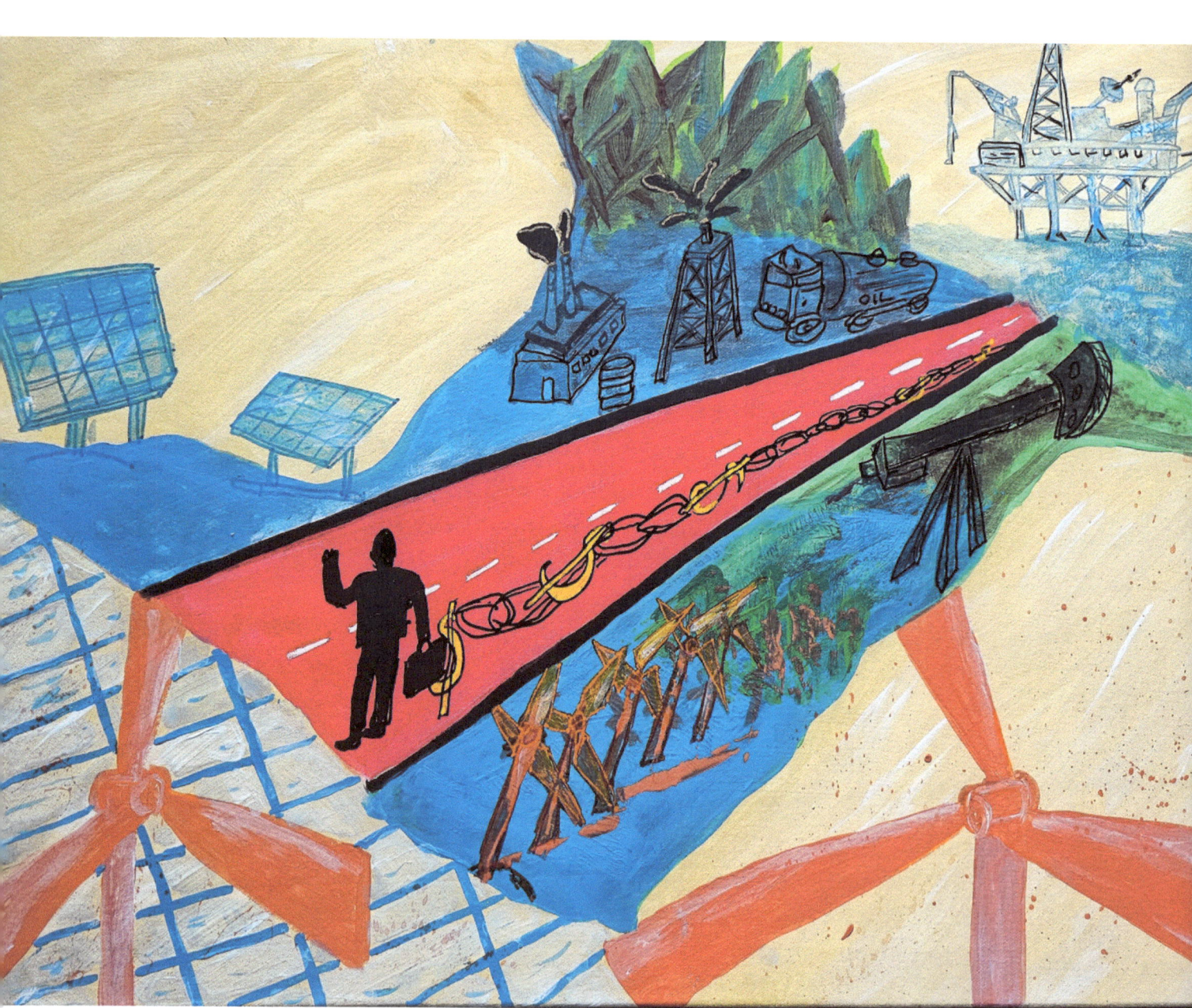

Pollution

Mikhaela Browne

"It was Easter 2023," Grandma began, "School had just closed, and my sisters and I would rush out into the backyard of our house. We would trample through the teak forest with only the sound of the brown, dry leaves crunching beneath our sneakers. Radiant, coloured butterflies with wings like canvases fluttered from flower to flower in a cheerful way. We would race to the sugar mango tree, plucking the rosy, red fruit from the branches, then biting into it as the yellow juice trickled down our elbows. We would then venture to the pond and dip our feet in and laugh as the puny fish nibbled on our toes." Grandma sighed tilting her head backward, her eyes hazing over as she seemed to be lost in her memories.

Simon looked at his grandmother rocking back and forth in her chair. He loved when grandma told stories from her childhood and longed to experience those days when there was grass and the rivers were clean. He wished to taste the sweet nectar of mango. But that was all in the past. Simon ventured to the back door of his grandmother's house. He cracked open the door only to be greeted by the stench of smoke and had to immediately strap on an oxygen mask to his face as the air was no longer safe to breathe. The forest was long gone, replaced with a housing development and a factory puffed out thick onyx smoke into the once azul sky. No creatures hopped around or any butterflies fluttered. No birds sang from the treetops. The pond was filled with cement and all the fishes had been lost. The once beautiful evening sun was covered in smoke.

Simon wished he had a time machine. If he had one, he'd go back to 2023 and tell all those people, "Listen, I am from the future, 2093, and in the future the world is polluted and destroyed. We must not cut the trees down. Trees provide habitats for hummingbirds, iguanas, ocelots, and agoutis. Trees provide shade and help with climate change by taking in carbon dioxide. He would tell the people to reduce the use of fossil fuels and use sustainable fuel sources such as solar and wind energy. In 2093, the air is so polluted it isn't safe to breathe in anymore. Do you want to have to walk around with an oxygen tank on your back. That is why we must protect the earth.

Just Change

Sai Sonali Anmolsingh

Somewhere on the island
A tree planted new roots
And an army of seedlings went from one nation
To a rebirth born from deforestation.
We were close once when
I gifted you clouds and
Let mist drip like mother's milk from hilltops
Laden with sweet fruit kisses and solar hugs.
That just changed
When you changed to the foil in this plot-
Yes, you toiled with your own hands,
But you made indigo soil boil,
Unrefined oil bubbling hot in a pot
Until acres of oceans were one sweaty drop
That let my flat bald head shine like tin,
Didn't matter that I bawled, and teardrops waved on land
When you plucked every brown strand
And you ignored me when I tried to take a stand.
Tree vines died and came alive
Turned into charcoal cables tracing roads in the sky
So trees' branches could birth franchises and
Where my loving tears trailed was filled with pails of pitch,
Sewage systems made out of every river, stream, ditch
As if nature was the real glitch,
Part of an unscratchable itch to switch,
An Itch for loose change,
You know better than to just monetize change.
Since when did mothers spend time in time out?

The roots in my heart pine because
It's hard to reach out when I am so confined.
Despite all the letters I scribbled on ochre pages,
Etched on cliff faces that linger through the ages,
Every year you pen me less.
I sit alone, smoke bush to burn stress.
The sun presses me when she comes knocking for you
And I choke on scorpion pepper anger-
She eclipses with shame when you shave a dollar from me
To save for fleeting philosophies in comedy shows
When you treat justice like jests,
Mountainous jokes in the valleys of inequity,
Where I show you showers,
Feelings, tears, sweat, blood
And you still laugh until it's your home in the flood.
Your corbeau-coloured constructions
Bringing your own destruction
And you shout for someone else
To deliver a just change.
My own blood doesn't care about anything's welfare
When all that matters is planting the seeds of power in warfare.
Somehow, each time my heart heavies, cloudbursts, fears,
You grow, everchanging in a place of rebirth,
Earth that thrives in the adverse.
So I let the wind carry cotton microphones
To play plea songs for my children
Because I know deep in the shifting plates at my core
You grow from roots wise and wild
Stem from starry seeds of change
And under umber leaves where your eyes should see
You aren't as blind as you pretend to be.
To make a change, pick your own heart and mind
Instead of digging out mines
And just change.

Sai Sonali Anmolsingh

The Focal Point

Jayda Ramjattan

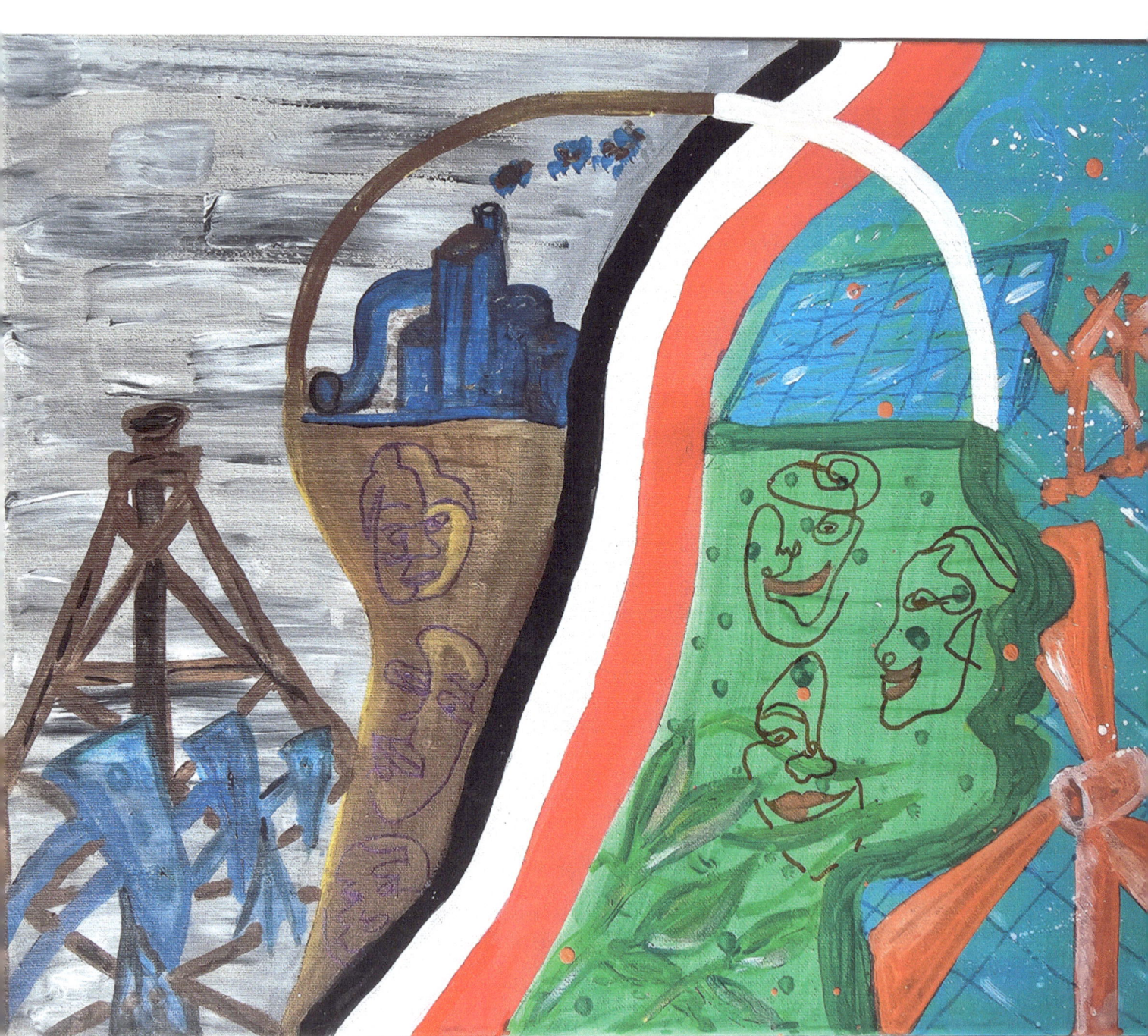

You feel that Heat?

Semira Bradshaw

I feeling hot hot hot
Yesss me too
But what really can we do
We are the ones affecting our environment and we acting like we have no
CLUE
Burning of fossil fuels, littering and cutting down trees, all our non renewable
and renewable resources being abuse
So what to do
We should be a-shame
We just polluting and adding to the climate change over and over again
You don't find it strange
Is like the sun fed up of the pollution, that he just fuming with RAGE these
days
I don't blame him.
We not doing our Job but want to fete and party like the climate is normal
Come on Trinidad and Tobago we can do better than this
I really think so
Let's impact our environment positively,
with planting a tree,
riding a bicycle,
Let's conserve our water and energy
And God will continue to be A TRINI
So let's not search for change but let's come together and Be the Change.

Just Transition Trinidad and Tobago!

Katrina Khan-Roberts

We know the science,
We see the signs,
But what are we to do,
When other issues cloud our minds?
We live off of oil and gas,
Our energy is relatively cheap,
But now as prices are increasing,
Our first response is to weep.
We must adopt the solution,
We must look to change,
We can't quietly continue,
As the weather becomes more strange
What are we waiting for?
Why do we hem and haw?
Why can't we support the just transition?
Why can't we update the law?
Why don't we learn about solar and wind?
Let's research the renewable tech.
We have tools at our disposal,
Not only a hand, we have the whole deck.
Our decision makers will continue
Continuing what they do,
If we don't hold them accountable
To look at the state anew.
It is going to take all of us,
Our collective understanding and choice.
We have what we need for the just transition,
We just have to unify our voice.

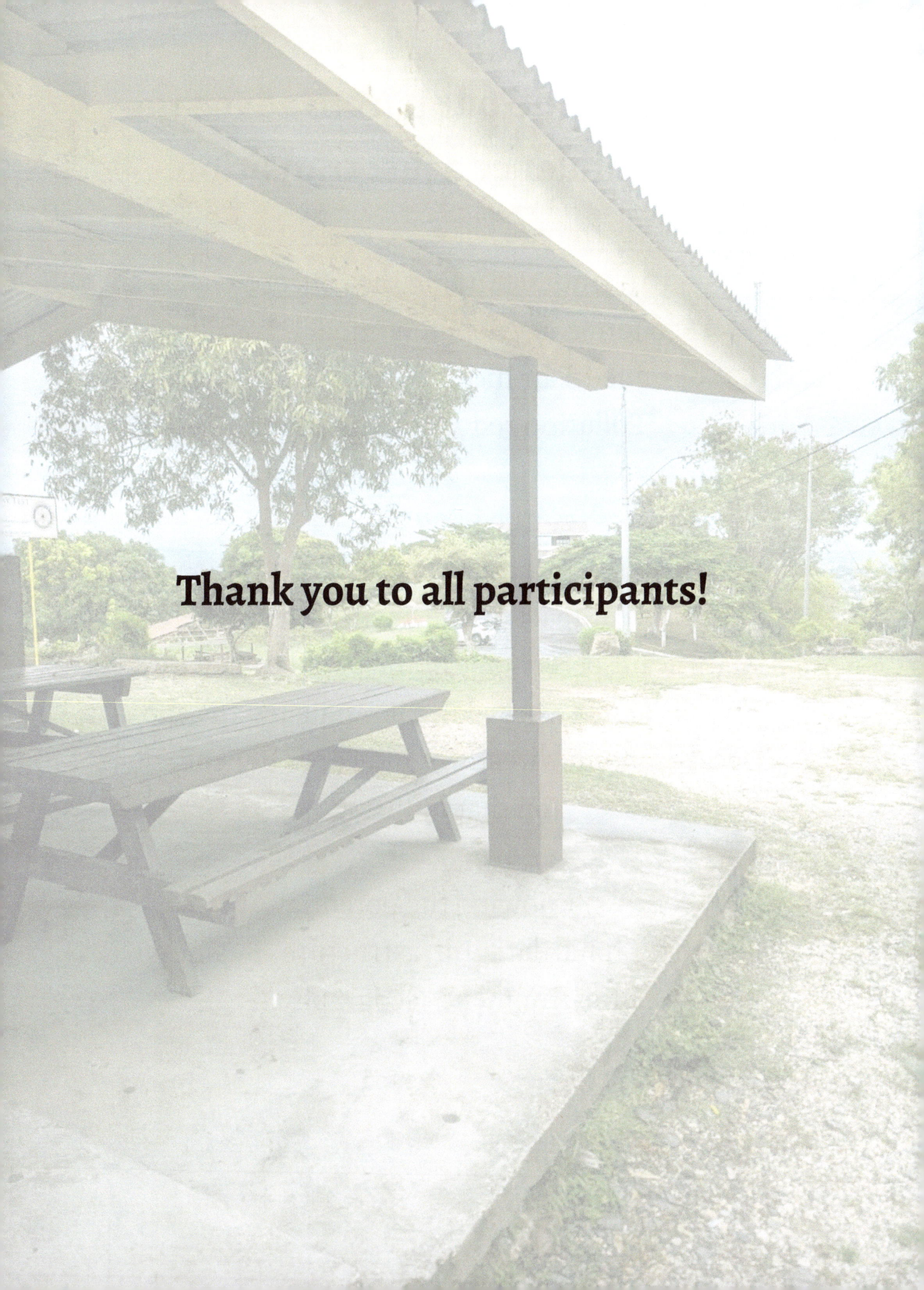

Thank you to all participants!

We can all do our part to advocate and influence a just transition:

1. Understanding the concept
Economic development model, Locally designed,Fair income and a decent life, Pollution reduction measures.

2. Choosing an area
The existence of a dominant industry which has a negative impact on the environment where a significant percentage of the population which works or has worked in that industry and the local economy directly or indirectly dependent on that industry

3. Knowing the potential
Demographic data, Infrastructure, Business Environment, Geography,

4. Decision-maker agreement

Leaders understand local realities; they confer legitimacy because they are appointed to represent the interests of citizens; they own the tools to implement community agreed measures; they have expertise.

5. Community consultation

every person living near the area in which these companies operate, regardless of age, gender, occupation, political or religious affiliation etc. All opinions are welcome because one of the defining principles for a just transition is its development from the bottom up.

6. Success stories

The concept of just transition is new, the need for economic alternatives in regions which relied on underground resources has existed in the past. We do not want to reinvent the wheel, but to use what we find useful in examples.

7. Support

Power of decision and the necessary resources are concentrated at the national level. Promoting a legislative project involves a lengthy endeavour and a correlated push of all local actors, investment and education.

8. Financial instruments

The revenues intended for just transition will be used in different ways, such as:

- Educational / training initiatives for requalifying workers
- Support job-seeking
- Businesses development

9. Re-Evaluation

To change the future sustainably, a long-term continuous effort is needed.

Types of Renewable Energy

SOLAR ENERGY

WIND ENERGY

GEOTHERMAL ENERGY

HYDROPOWER

OCEAN ENERGY

BIOENERGY

Notes

Notes

List of Contributors

Hassan Voyeau

Heidi Boodoosingh

Mikhaela Browne

Davi Ramkallawan

Ryan Bachoo

I-yana Dinzey

Lee-Marie Preston

Ayesha Rivers

Myalee Phillip

Jayda Ramjattan

Sai Sonali Anmolsingh

Semira Bradshaw

Katrina Khan-Roberts

Event Photos
Friday November 3rd 2023

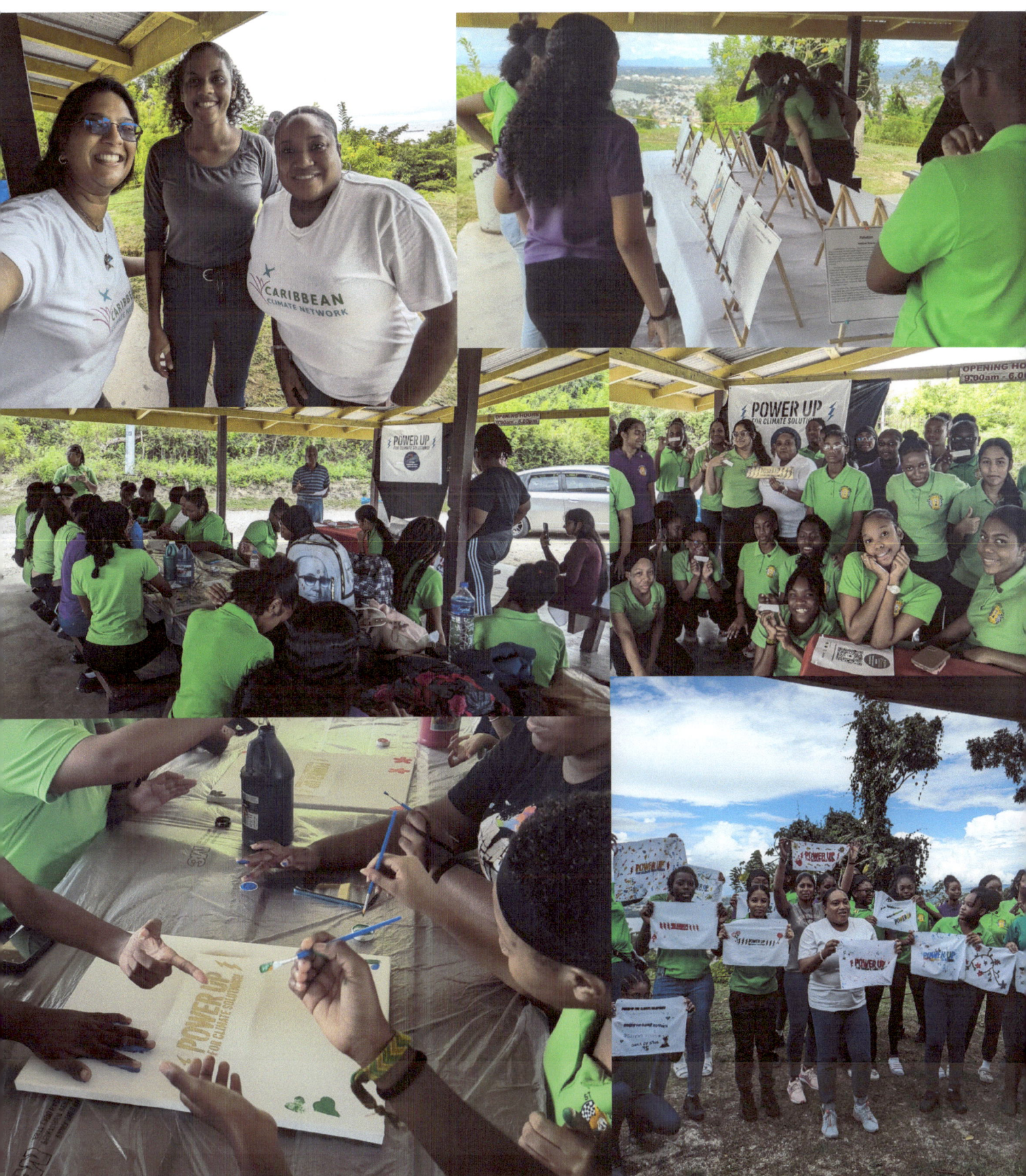

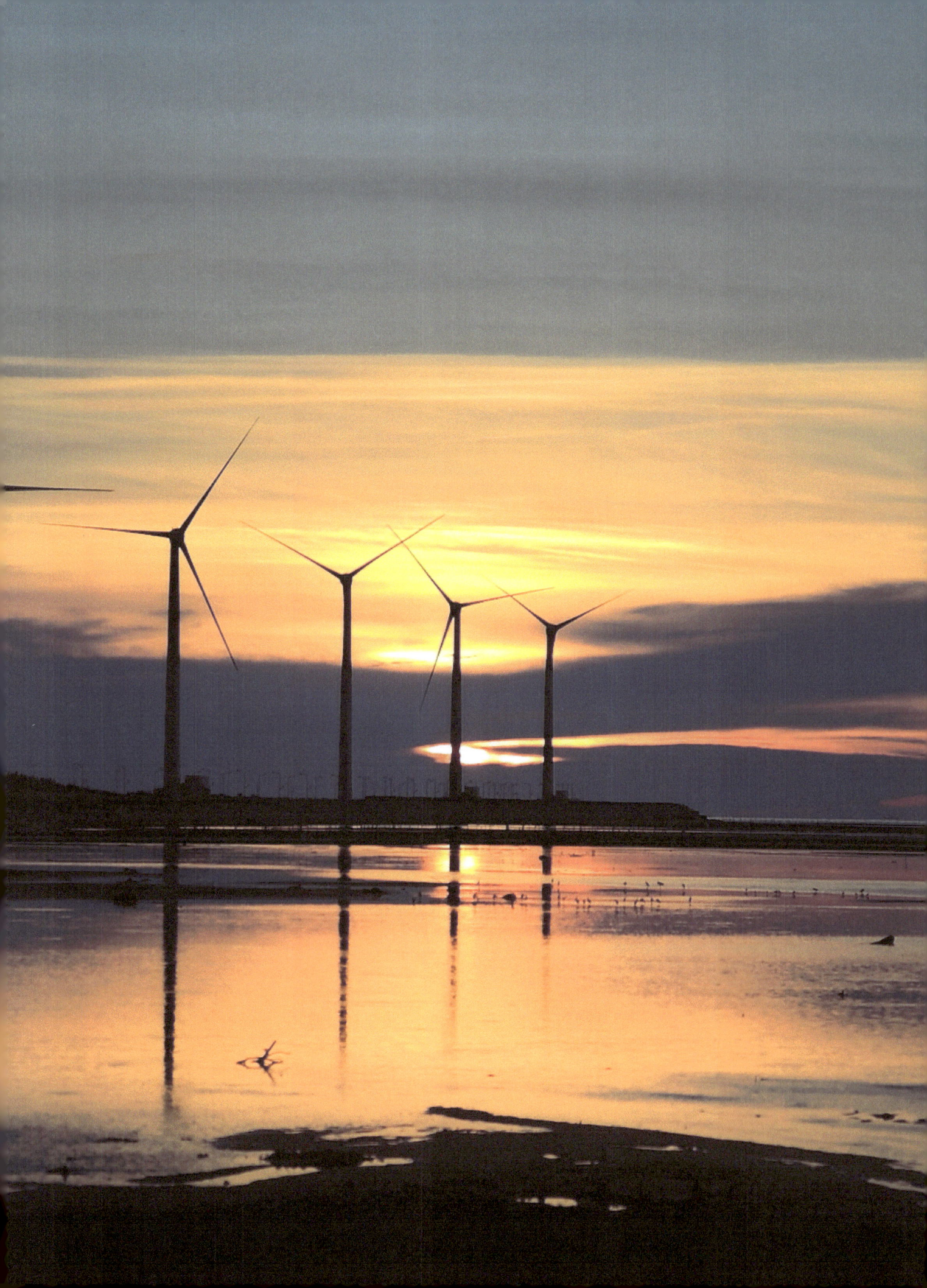